Start Your Small Business with AI

The Super Beginner's Step-by-Step Guide to Building a Profitable Business with Zero Experience, No Tech Skills, and Smart AI Help Along the Way

Written by
Eric LeBouthillier

AcraSolution | 2025 1st Edition
www.acrasolution.com

Preface

Starting a business can feel scary — especially if you're not a "business person" or don't understand technology. I get it. I've been there.

This book was written for people who want to start something of their own — but don't know where to begin, what steps to take, or how to keep from getting overwhelmed.

Here's the good news:
You don't need to have it all figured out.
You don't need to be a tech expert.
You don't even need a big idea yet.

You just need a little guidance — and a smart assistant. That's where this book (and a bit of AI) comes in.

We'll take it step by step. Slowly. Clearly. Together.
You'll learn how to build a real business from the ground up — one that fits your life, your pace, and your goals. And you'll use easy AI tools to make the whole process smoother.

Let's get started — one page at a time.

— Eric LeBouthillier
Author & Cybersecurity Strategist

For permission requests or inquiries, contact the publisher through the website : www.acrasolution.com

LEGAL DISCLAIMER

This eBook is provided for informational purposes only and does not constitute legal, financial, or professional advice. The author and publisher have made every reasonable effort to ensure the accuracy and completeness of the information contained herein; however, neither assumes any responsibility for errors, omissions, or contrary interpretations of the subject matter.

Readers are encouraged to consult with qualified professionals for specific advice tailored to their individual needs. The mention of any products, services, or third-party entities does not imply an endorsement or guarantee of their effectiveness or suitability. Any application of the strategies and recommendations presented is at the reader's discretion and risk.

The author and publisher shall not be liable for any damages (including, without limitation, direct, indirect, incidental, or consequential) caused by the use, misuse, or interpretation of the information herein. All references to regulatory standards, statutes, or compliance requirements are informational and do not replace official legal counsel.

By reading and applying the concepts in this eBook, you acknowledge that you bear sole responsibility for the outcomes of your decisions and actions. If you do not agree to these terms, please discontinue use of this publication immediately.

Table of Contents

Who This Book Is For

This book is for you if:

- You've never started a business before — and don't know where to start
- You feel overwhelmed by all the tools, terms, and tech people talk about
- You learn better with clear steps, simple language, and zero pressure
- You want to build something small, honest, and profitable
- You've heard about AI and want to know how it can *actually* help you
- You've been dreaming of working for yourself, but you've been stuck in "what if" mode

This is not a book for business pros.
It's for first-timers. Side-hustlers. Slow learners. Creators who are ready to try.

If that's you — welcome.
This book was written with *you* in mind.

Chapter 1: You Can Do This — Even If You Know Nothing (Yet)

Introduction

Let's start with this simple truth: *You don't need to be an expert to start a business.* You don't need an MBA, a perfect idea, or a background in technology. All you need is the willingness to learn, try, and take small steps forward. That's it.

This chapter is here to hold your hand, quiet your doubts, and remind you that you're not alone. You might feel unsure or even a little scared. That's totally normal. The good news? You're in the right place — and you're starting at the best possible time.

Why Now Is the Best Time Ever to Start Your Own Business

There has *never* been a better time in history to start something of your own. Why?

- You don't need a lot of money to begin.
- You don't need to rent an office or hire a big team.
- You don't need a fancy website or a technical degree.

Thanks to simple tools (including AI), you can run an entire business from your phone, your kitchen table, or even your local coffee shop.

The world has changed. People *want* more flexibility. They trust small, personal brands. They shop online. They look for real people solving real problems — not just big companies with big ads.

You're not late to the game. You're actually early to a brand-new one.

What's Different Now?

- **Tech tools are easier than ever.** Many are made for beginners and explain every step.
- **AI (like ChatGPT) is your helper.** It can give you ideas, write for you, and even help build things.
- **You can reach people instantly.** Social media and online platforms let you connect with customers from day one.
- **Micro-businesses are thriving.** You don't need to build the next Amazon. You just need to solve one little problem for one group of people.

Starting small is smart. Starting *now* is even smarter.

Busting the "I'm Not Ready" and "I'm Not Technical" Myths

Let's talk about the two biggest lies that stop people from ever getting started:

"I'm Not Ready"

You don't need to "feel ready." Most people *never* feel fully ready — even the ones who succeed later.

Fact: The only real way to get ready… is to begin.

The first step might feel awkward or messy. That's okay. Every confident entrepreneur you see today started with zero experience and a whole lot of guesswork.

What matters is showing up. Trying. Learning. You're doing that right now.

"I'm Not Technical"

Guess what? You don't have to be.

We're not building robots or writing code here. We're starting simple, helpful businesses — and AI tools can now do most of the technical stuff *for* you.

Think of AI as your friendly assistant. It can:

- Help you brainstorm names, taglines, and business ideas
- Write emails, product descriptions, or social media posts
- Give you step-by-step instructions for tasks you've never done before

If you can type and click, you can use AI.

And if anything feels confusing? That's what this book is for. We're going to walk you through everything.

What AI Is — And How It Will Help You Along the Way

Let's get this part nice and simple:

AI (Artificial Intelligence) is just a smart tool that helps you get things done faster, easier, and with less stress. It's like a super-powered digital assistant that never sleeps.

AI won't replace your creativity, your heart, or your unique ideas — but it *will* make the process a lot smoother.

Here's what AI can do for you in your new business:

- **Speed up your work:** Need to write a blog post, create a checklist, or outline a product? AI can help you finish it in minutes.
- **Fill in your knowledge gaps:** Don't know how to do something? Ask the AI. It can explain things in plain English, step by step.
- **Save you money:** Instead of hiring a writer, designer, or marketer right away, you can get started using AI tools for free or very cheap.
- **Help you feel more confident:** You'll never be stuck staring at a blank screen or wondering "what do I do next?" — AI is always there with suggestions and support.

Think of it like this: AI is your business buddy. You bring the ideas, the care, the passion. AI brings the tools.

Simple Checklist: Are You Willing to Learn, Try, and Take Baby Steps?

Before we go any further, let's check in with where you are right now. If you can honestly say "yes" to most of these questions, you're absolutely ready to start.

- ☑ I'm curious about starting something of my own
- ☑ I'm open to learning new things (even if I feel a little nervous)
- ☑ I'm willing to make mistakes and keep going anyway
- ☑ I like the idea of helping people and making money doing it
- ☑ I'm not expecting overnight success — just excited to try
- ☑ I'd love a little guidance and support (thanks, book!)

If that's you — welcome. You are *exactly* the kind of person who can make this work.

And if you're still unsure? That's okay too. Stick with us. We're going to make this journey simple, encouraging, and completely doable.

Common Myths That Stop People from Starting

- "I don't have a big idea." You don't need one (yet).
- "I don't know where to start." You're here. That's the start.
- "I'm not a business person." Neither was anyone... until they started one.
- "I might fail." That's just part of learning. We all fail our way to success.

Every expert was once a beginner. Every thriving business started as a tiny spark.

Real-World Example: Meet Kayla, the Accidental Entrepreneur

What happened:
Kayla was a stay-at-home mom who loved organizing birthday parties for her kids. One day, a friend asked if she could help plan a party for their niece. Then another friend asked. Then someone offered to pay her.

She didn't think she was "ready" or "qualified." But she used ChatGPT to:

- Help write her first service description
- Create a logo and business name
- Plan a simple pricing page
- Build her first customer email reply

She made her first $250 in just one week.

What went right:

- She started small, with what she already liked doing.
- She used AI to fill in the blanks.
- She focused on *helping*, not "selling."

What we learn:

- You don't need to wait.
- You don't need to have it all figured out.
- AI makes starting a business 10× easier than it used to be.

You don't have to be perfect. You just have to begin.

In the next chapter, we'll explore something a lot of people misunderstand: **What exactly *is* a business?**

You'll learn the difference between products, services, and content — and which one might be perfect for *you*. Spoiler alert: You'll be surprised how easy it is to start offering value with what you already know or enjoy.

Let's keep going — you're doing great.

Chapter 2: What Is a Business? (The Simplest Explanation Ever)

Introduction

Before you start a business, it helps to know what a business *actually is*. Not in a textbook way. In a real, simple, "I can do this" kind of way.

You might picture a business as a store, a logo, a website, or a big company with employees. But that's not the full story. At its core, a business is much simpler:

A business is just a way to help people — and get paid for it.

That's it. That's the heart of it. You help someone solve a problem, enjoy something, or make life easier… and they give you money in return.

Whether you're selling cookies, organizing closets, or teaching people how to play guitar — it's all business.

Let's break it down into the easiest explanation ever.

What Does It *Really* Mean to Have a Business?

A business is not about being fancy, perfect, or popular. It's about creating *value* — something useful, helpful, entertaining, or meaningful — and getting *paid* for it.

Here's what that looks like in real life:

- You **solve a problem** someone is willing to pay for
- You **offer something** that makes someone's life better
- You **deliver it** in a way that feels good and trustworthy

And guess what? You don't need a huge audience, a perfect brand, or even a website to begin. Many successful businesses start with just:

- A clear offer
- One way for people to find you
- One way for people to pay you

Think of It Like This…

If someone pays you to bake a cake, walk their dog, build a simple website, or write a newsletter — that's already a business.

If you create videos or guides or artwork that others want to buy or subscribe to — that's also a business.

It's not about size. It's about *value exchange* — helping in a way that matters enough for people to say: "Yes, that's worth paying for."

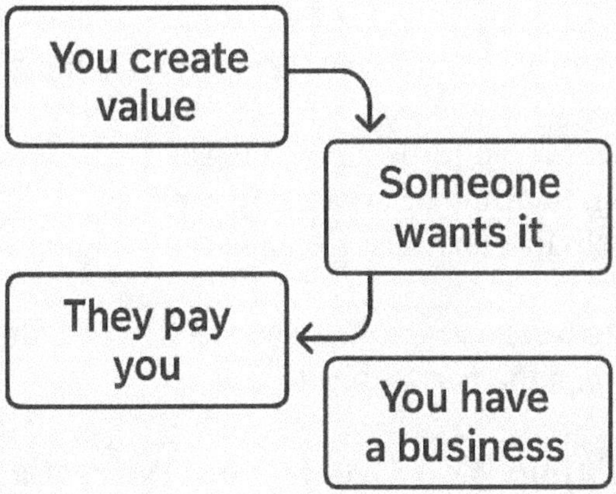

Product vs. Service vs. Content — What Can You Sell?

Let's look at the three easiest types of businesses for beginners. You can start with just one.

1. Products – Things People Can Buy

This is something *tangible* or *digital* that people can purchase. It could be:

- A handmade item (like candles, crafts, baked goods)
- A digital file (like templates, eBooks, or planners)
- A physical product you ship or dropship

With AI tools, you can even create digital products — like journals, printable coloring books, or guides — without being a designer.

2. Services – Things You Do for Others

This is where you offer your time or skills. For example:

- Social media help for local businesses
- Pet sitting, tutoring, or organizing services
- Admin help like answering emails or setting up calendars

You don't need to be an expert. You just need to be a little better (or more available) than the person hiring you.

3. Content – Things You Create That Attract an Audience

Content is where you share your ideas, stories, tips, or entertainment — and grow a following. You can eventually earn through:

- Sponsorships
- Paid subscriptions
- Selling your own products or services to that audience

Examples include:

- YouTube channels
- Newsletters
- Podcasts
- Social media pages

Don't worry — you don't need to go viral. Even a small, loyal audience can be the start of a thriving business.

Real Examples of Beginner-Friendly Businesses

Let's take a look at a few real, simple businesses that started small:

Example 1: The Etsy Mom

Maria started making cute baby headbands for her daughter. Friends loved them. She opened an Etsy shop. AI helped her write product listings and name her store. She now makes $400–$800 a month, part-time.

Example 2: The Local Helper

Josh offered to help his neighbor organize her garage. She told a friend. That friend told two more. He used AI to write a flyer and print it out. Now he's booked most weekends and saves for his first car.

Example 3: The Content Creator

Sophie loves books. She started posting short reviews on TikTok. People began following her. She used AI to help plan video ideas. Now she earns through affiliate links and a small book-themed email newsletter.

What do all three have in common?

- They started with something they already liked or were good at
- They used simple tools (including AI) to look more "official"
- They kept it small and manageable — one step at a time

AI Tool: Ask ChatGPT for 5 Simple Business Model Ideas Based on Your Interests

Let's try something fun and helpful.

Open ChatGPT and type something like:

"Give me 5 simple, beginner-friendly business ideas I can start based on someone who loves [insert your interest]."

Examples:

- …who loves dogs
- …who enjoys organizing
- …who's good at writing
- …who wants to work from home

Here's what AI might return:

1. Start a dog walking or pet-sitting business
2. Offer home organization services for busy parents
3. Write blog posts or product descriptions for small businesses
4. Create printable planners or checklists on Etsy
5. Start a simple email newsletter about something you enjoy

You don't have to pick one yet. Just explore. Get curious. See what sounds fun and possible.

Action Steps: Your Beginner Business Thinking Cap

Here's a quick exercise to warm up your business brain:

1. Think of 3 things you love to do
(e.g., baking, writing, fixing things, helping people)

2. Think of 3 things people have asked you for help with
(e.g., tech help, advice, decorating, errands)

3. Ask AI to combine those ideas into business models
Prompt:

"Based on someone who loves [your answers] and has helped others with [your answers], what are 3 business ideas they could try?"

You might be surprised at how doable it all feels when you see it in writing.

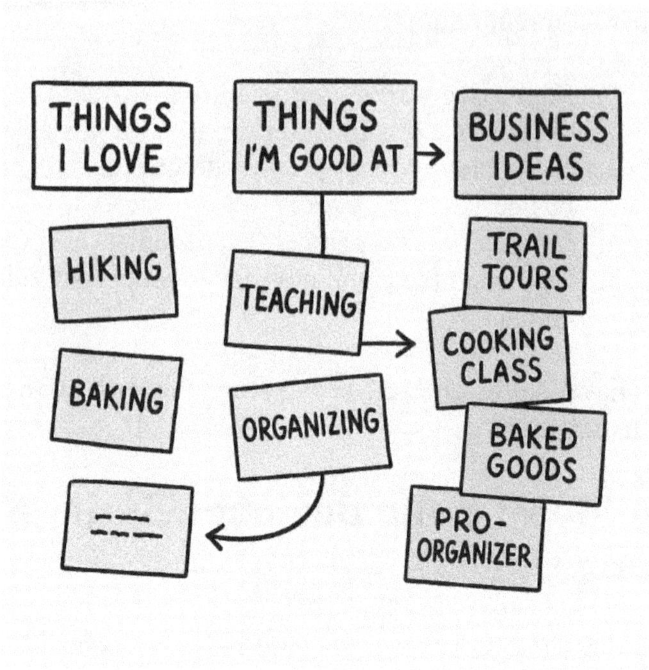

You're not supposed to have it all figured out yet. You're supposed to *start exploring.*

In the next chapter, we'll go deeper into how to find a simple, profitable business idea that actually fits you — your skills, your life, and your interests.

You'll also learn how to use AI to test and refine your ideas *before* you spend a single dollar.

Let's go from "maybe" to "let's try."

NEXT STEPS

- Understand that a business is just helping + getting paid
- Pick one path to explore: product, service, or content
- Use AI to brainstorm business models based on your interests
- Look at real beginner stories — yours can start the same way
- Don't overthink — stay playful and curious

Next up: Chapter 3 — Finding a Simple, Profitable Business Idea
We'll help you connect what you're good at with what people need — and how to use AI to find and shape your best-fit business idea.

Chapter 3: Finding a Simple, Profitable Business Idea

Introduction

You've got the courage. You're curious. You're open to learning. Now comes the fun part: figuring out *what kind* of business you might actually want to start.

But don't worry — this isn't about chasing the next big trend or guessing what might make money. It's about matching who *you already are* with what *other people need.*

That sweet spot — where your skills, interests, and someone else's problem all come together — is where your business can begin.

Let's make this simple, clear, and confidence-boosting.

Brainstorming With Purpose: What Are You Good At? What Do People Need?

Forget the pressure of having "the perfect idea." Most great businesses start small — with something the founder already enjoys, notices, or is naturally helpful at.

Start With You

Here are a few prompts to unlock business-worthy skills and interests:

- What do people often ask you for help with?
- What do you enjoy doing that feels easy or fun?
- What kind of tasks or topics do you lose track of time doing?
- Have you solved a problem in your own life that others might also face?

Your first business doesn't have to be your *forever* business. It just has to start somewhere that feels right — for you.

Then Think About Others

Now flip the script:

- What are people complaining about lately?
- What feels harder than it should be for others?
- What do your friends or family struggle to figure out?
- What do *you* wish existed (that you could create or offer)?

Business happens when you match a "you" answer with a "them" need.

Here's a cheat sheet to mix and match:

YOU Love This	**THEY Need Help With**	**Possible Idea**
Taking photos	Social media posts	$25/month content packs
Being organized	Decluttering their homes	Simple home reset service
Writing tips	Creating bios or blogs	AI-aided writing services
Finding deals	Saving money	Newsletter or digital guide

The "One-Person Business" Mindset

Let's clear something up: You don't need to build a company with staff, investors, or offices.

You can build a *One-Person Business* that runs from your laptop or phone — with low costs, flexible hours, and total creative control.

A One-Person Business is:

- Simple to start
- Easy to scale (if you want)
- Focused on value and service — not complexity
- Often more *profitable* than big, stressful operations

This mindset frees you to:

- Start lean (no big spending)
- Move fast (try things out, learn quickly)
- Keep things fun and personal

Think of yourself as a *value creator* with tools (like AI) and platforms (like Etsy, Gumroad, Substack, etc.) doing the heavy lifting.

Validating Your Idea Using AI + Real-World Search

Once you have a few possible business ideas, you don't need to *guess* which one works best. You can *test* it — quickly, easily, and affordably.

Step 1: Ask AI for Feedback

Use a prompt like:

"I'm thinking of starting a business where I [describe your idea]. Can you help me think through the pros, cons, and how people might react to this?"

ChatGPT can help you:

- Spot potential challenges
- Suggest better ways to phrase your offer
- Highlight who might need your service or product

Step 2: Do a Real-World Mini-Search

Here's what to look up online:

- Are people already looking for this?
  Search phrases like: *"how to [your idea]"* or *"best [your topic] for beginners"*
- Are others doing it? That's a good sign! Competition = demand
- Are there reviews or comments? What do people wish was better?

You're not trying to find a perfect idea. You're checking:

- Is this helpful?
- Does it already exist (in some form)?
- Can I offer a slightly different or more personal version?

No demand = danger. But *some* competition = opportunity.

AI Tool: Generate 10 Beginner-Friendly Business Ideas + Refine With Prompts

Here's where AI becomes your creative business buddy.

Try this prompt in ChatGPT:

"Give me 10 simple business ideas someone could start with no budget, based on a love for [insert your interests or skills], and a goal to help others."

Examples:

- ...a love for writing and helping others organize
- ...a knack for chatting and giving advice
- ...an interest in design and personal growth

You'll get a brainstormed list of doable, small-start ideas.

Now, refine it.

Take your favorite one and ask:

"Can you turn this into a 3-step starter plan?"
"Who would be the ideal customer for this?"
"What kind of name or brand might fit this?"

Suddenly, you're not guessing — you're shaping.

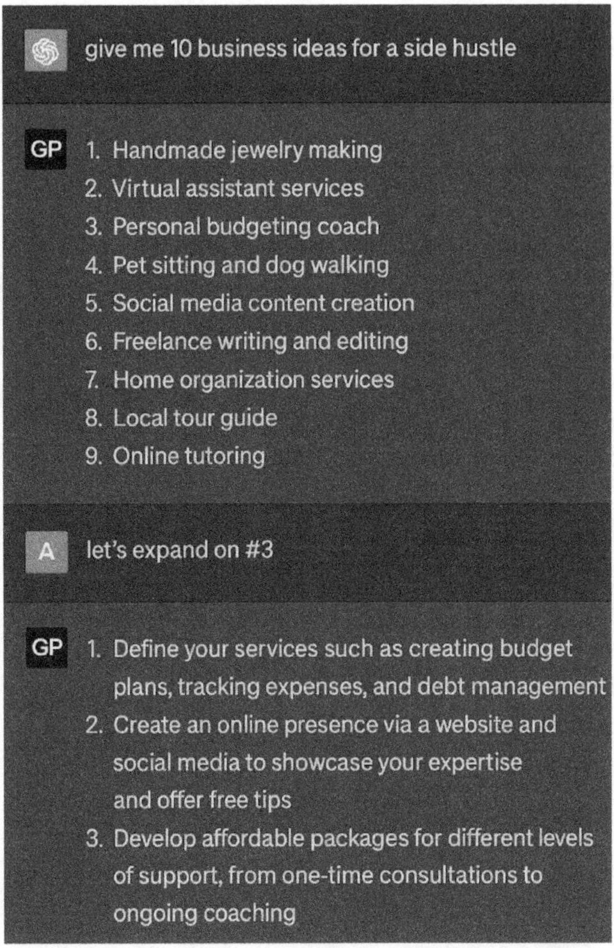

Real-World Example: Tony's "Tiny Tech Help" Idea

What happened:
Tony was good with computers — nothing fancy, just fixing slow Wi-Fi or helping people set up their email. He started offering "Tiny Tech Help" to seniors in his neighborhood.

AI helped him:

- Come up with the name and tagline
- Write a simple flyer
- List the top 10 things he could help with

His first client gave him a $20 tip and told five friends. Within a month, Tony had made over $1,000 — all from helping people with small tech headaches.

What went right:

- He started with what he was already good at
- He kept the idea tiny and clear
- AI gave him momentum without overthinking

What we learn:

- Business ideas don't have to be big
- Start with what feels natural
- AI helps you go from idea → action, fast

You're not looking for a perfect idea. You're looking for a *good enough* idea to start with.

In the next chapter, we'll answer a critical question: **Do people actually want what you're offering?**

It's not enough to like your idea — others need to *want it too*. We'll show you exactly how to check for real-world demand using Google, forums, reviews, and of course… AI.

NEXT STEPS

- Brainstorm from what you enjoy + what people need
- Embrace the "One-Person Business" path — it's powerful
- Use AI to shape and test your top ideas
- Validate through real searches, not just gut feelings
- Choose one idea to explore in more depth

Next up: Chapter 4 — Is There Demand for My Idea? (Don't Skip This)
Let's make sure your idea is something people *want* — before you build anything.

Chapter 4: Is There Demand for My Idea? (Don't Skip This)

Introduction

You've got a fun, doable business idea — or maybe even a few. But before you start building a website, printing business cards, or posting on social media, you need to answer one crucial question:

Do people *actually* want this?

Many new businesses fail not because the person lacked talent or effort, but because… no one wanted what they were offering.

But don't worry — we're not guessing here. You're going to learn *exactly* how to check for demand using simple tools like Google, Reddit, Amazon, and AI.

This chapter is like turning on a flashlight before walking through the woods. Let's make sure your idea has a clear path forward — with real people ready and waiting.

How to Know If People Actually Want Your Offer

Here's a truth that might surprise you:

A "great idea" is only great if someone's willing to pay for it.

The goal here isn't perfection — it's *proof of interest.* You want to see if people are already searching for, asking about, or complaining about the very problem you're aiming to solve.

Quick Demand Checks

Ask yourself:

- Are people *already paying* for similar things?
- Are they talking about this topic in forums or comment sections?
- Are they asking questions that your business could answer?

If yes, that's *very* good news. You don't need to be the first — you just need to show up and offer value in a way that's *you.*

Google Search Tips, Reddit/Forums, Amazon Digging

These free tools are your best friends for real-world research. Here's how to use them:

Google Search

Go to Google and type in phrases related to your idea:

- "How to fix [problem your business solves]"
- "Best [product/service] for beginners"
- "Affordable [your niche] help"

Pay attention to:

- **Auto-complete suggestions** — these show what people commonly type
- **People also ask** sections — these are real questions being asked
- **Related searches** at the bottom — a goldmine for phrasing and trends

Reddit and Forums

Visit Reddit.com and search for topics like:

- "struggling with [your idea's focus]"
- "need help with [problem you solve]"
- "recommend a good [type of business or product]"

You'll often find honest, unfiltered pain points — and your chance to serve them better.

Amazon Reviews

Look at books or products in your area and read the **1-star and 3-star reviews**. Why?

- 5-star = happy
- 1-star = angry
- 3-star = *room for improvement* — this is your window!

Example:

Someone leaves a review on a budgeting workbook: "Great idea, but too complicated for beginners."
You could create: **A super-simple, AI-powered version.**

AI Tool: ChatGPT + Google Trends to Scan Demand and Competition

Use AI to help you pull together what the research is showing.

Here's a simple workflow:

Step 1: Ask ChatGPT for Demand Insights

Try this prompt:

"I'm considering a business that helps [target audience] with [problem or need]. Can you tell me how common this issue is, and what people might be searching for?"

Follow up with:

"What kinds of products or services are already being offered in this space?"

ChatGPT will give you a starting landscape of competition, gaps, and opportunities.

Step 2: Use Google Trends

Go to trends.google.com and search keywords from your idea:

- "Meal planning for busy moms"
- "Pet photography services"
- "Budget travel guides"

You'll see:

- Search volume over time (is it growing?)
- Regional interest (where is it hot?)
- Related rising queries (hidden gems!)

This combo helps you avoid the trap of launching into something *you* love… but no one else wants.

Exercise: Ask AI to Summarize Your Target Audience in 3 Bullet Points

Knowing who you're serving makes everything clearer — your website, your tone, your pricing, even your logo.

Try this:

"Based on my business idea: [describe it], who is my ideal target audience? Can you describe them in 3 simple bullet points?"

Example:

Business idea: "Helping busy parents plan affordable, healthy meals using AI-generated grocery lists."

ChatGPT might return:

- Parents aged 28–45 juggling work, kids, and meal prep
- Frustrated by planning, but want better food choices
- Looking for easy, budget-friendly solutions they can trust

These three points become the backbone of your messaging, branding, and offers.

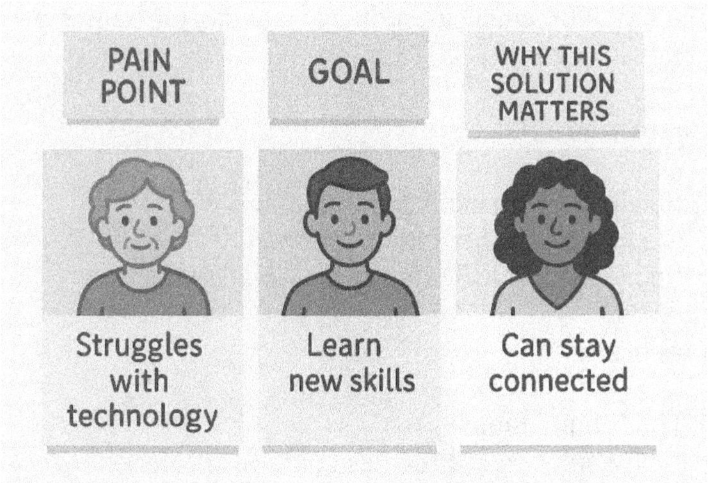

Real-World Example: Jen's AI Meal Plan Service

What happened:
Jen loved meal planning and healthy eating. She thought about selling pre-made grocery lists and recipes. Before she launched anything, she searched Google for "easy dinner plan for moms" and browsed Reddit threads about picky eaters.

She found:

- *Tons* of questions from busy parents
- Frustrations with planning, shopping, and repeating meals
- A demand for something super-simple and fast

Jen used ChatGPT to:

- Summarize her audience
- Write sample blog posts and list features
- Create a lead magnet: "3 AI-Generated Meal Plans for Families (Under $75/week)"

Now she has 500+ email subscribers — and is pre-selling her first $25/month subscription.

What went right:

- She tested demand before building
- She listened to her future customers
- She let AI guide her messaging and structure

What we learn:

- Don't build blindly
- Let people's *real* struggles guide your offer
- AI + search tools give you a huge head start

Your idea might feel exciting — but real success starts when other people are excited *too*.

Before you build, brand, or launch, make sure the *demand* is there. It saves time, builds confidence, and helps you create something people truly want.

In the next chapter, we'll take your solid idea and give it a name, a personality, and a digital home. Yep — it's branding time (and we'll make it super fun and simple).

NEXT STEPS

- Use Google, Reddit, and Amazon to look for proof of interest
- Ask AI for insights, ideas, and competitor snapshots
- Try Google Trends to watch growth and patterns
- Summarize your ideal customer in 3 clear points
- Validate before you build — you'll move faster, with less stress

Next up: Chapter 5 — Naming, Branding, and Getting Your Domain (Made Easy)
You'll learn how to name your business, grab a domain, and even write your first tagline — all with the help of AI.

Chapter 5: Naming, Branding, and Getting Your Domain (Made Easy)

Introduction

So you've got a real idea that people actually want — now it's time to give it a name, a face, and a digital home.

Naming your business and creating a simple brand isn't about being clever, trendy, or perfect. It's about being *clear, findable,* and *rememberable*. And the best part? You don't need to be a designer or copywriter — because AI can help with all of it.

In this chapter, we'll show you exactly how to:

- Pick a great business name
- Use AI to brainstorm taglines and logo ideas
- Check if your domain name is available
- And put together a brand look and message that makes you proud

Let's bring your business to life.

Picking a Name That's Simple, Clear, and Available

Here's the truth about naming your business:

Simple beats clever. Clear beats cute.

You want a name that people can:

- Say out loud easily
- Spell without guessing
- Remember after hearing once
- Type into a browser or social media search bar without confusion

Best Practices for Naming

✓ Use real words or easy-to-pronounce combos
Bad: "Xyblez Solutions" — What does that even mean?
Better: "Quick Fix Organizing" — Clear and keyword-friendly

✓ Hint at what you do or the result you offer
Names that suggest a *benefit* stick better:

- "Happy Pup Walks"
- "Budget Meal Planner"
- "Calm Desk Coaching"

✓ Keep it short (ideally under 3 words)
It should fit in a logo, headline, and social bio without being squished.

AI Tool: Business Name + Logo Generators

You can use AI to brainstorm dozens of name ideas in seconds.

Try this ChatGPT prompt:

"Give me 15 simple business name ideas for a company that helps [audience] with [problem/solution]. Focus on names that are short, clear, and sound friendly."

Example Prompt:

"Give me name ideas for a digital product that helps busy moms plan affordable meals using AI."

Once you get a list, ask follow-up questions:

- "Which of these would be best for a blog-style website?"
- "Which name feels more modern vs. cozy?"
- "Can you pair these names with tagline ideas?"

Free Tools to Generate Name and Logo Combos

- **namelix.com** – Generates brand-style names and logos
- **looka.com** – Helps design logos + brand kits
- **shopify's business name generator** – Great for ecommerce or services

You don't need to pay for anything yet — just experiment and save what you like.

How to Check If Your Domain Is Available

Once you've found a name you love (or two or three options), check if the .com domain is available.

Use tools like:

- Namecheap.com
- GoDaddy.com
- Google Domains

You want a domain that matches your business name as closely as possible:

- great: **happyorganizing.com**
- good: **happyorganizingco.com** or **gethappyorganizing.com**
- avoid: random dashes or long, hard-to-remember versions

TIP: Grab your name on social media too — even if you don't plan to use it right away. It protects your brand for later.

Pro Move: Use AI to check name + domain + tagline combos in one flow:

"Here are three names I'm considering. Can you suggest a domain and tagline for each?"

Example:

Name: Calm Desk Coaching
Domain: calmdeskcoaching.com (available)
Tagline: "Declutter your space, clear your mind."

Bonus: Use AI to Write Your First Tagline or Elevator Pitch

Your **tagline** is a one-sentence version of what your business does.

It should answer:

- Who you help
- What you help them with
- The result they can expect

Example AI Prompt

"Can you write a simple tagline for a business that helps freelancers stay organized using AI tools?"

AI Output Might Be:

- "Less chaos, more clients."
- "AI-powered calm for your creative hustle."
- "Freelance smarter, not harder."

Want to go further?

Ask:

"Can you write a 30-second elevator pitch for my business idea that sounds friendly and clear?"

You'll get a polished, human-sounding summary you can use on your website, in your email bio, or even when talking to friends.

Real-World Example: Bella's Plant Care Startup

What happened:
Bella loved indoor plants. She noticed people kept asking her how to stop them from dying. She wanted to start a business around this passion, but didn't know where to begin.

She used ChatGPT to:

- Brainstorm names like "Happy Leaves," "Plant Pal," and "Rooted at Home"
- Create logo concepts using Looka
- Check domains and landed on **plantpalcare.com**
- Write a tagline: "Helping your houseplants (and confidence) grow."

Now she offers beginner-friendly care guides and mini video consults. It's personal, helpful — and it all started with a name.

What went right:

- Bella picked something *she* loved
- AI helped speed up branding and writing
- Her name and tagline speak directly to her ideal customer

You don't need to overthink branding. You just need to make it *easy to understand and remember.*

Use your name and message to invite people in. Make it feel warm, clear, and trustworthy — like a friendly storefront they can't wait to explore.

In the next chapter, we'll take all of your progress — idea, audience, offer, and brand — and turn it into a super simple, one-page business plan you can actually use.

NEXT STEPS

- Brainstorm names that are short, clear, and hint at what you offer
- Use AI and free tools to explore logos, taglines, and brand vibes
- Check for domain and social media availability
- Don't wait for "perfect" — pick something good and start sharing

Next up: Chapter 6 — Writing a One-Page Business Plan (With AI Help)
You'll skip the 20-page document and create a super clear, fill-in-the-blanks plan that actually gets used.

Chapter 6: Writing a One-Page Business Plan (With AI Help)

Introduction

You don't need a thick binder, a formal presentation, or a 20-page document to plan your business. In fact, most successful solopreneurs and small business owners start with something much simpler — a **one-page business plan**.

This short, focused plan isn't about impressing investors. It's about giving *you* clarity:

- What are you doing?
- Who are you helping?
- How will you make money?

With a little help from AI, you can write a clean, practical business plan in under an hour — even if you've never done anything like this before.

Let's walk through the structure, step by step.

Why You Don't Need a 20-Page Business Plan

Let's bust this myth right away:

You do *not* need a detailed business plan to start.

Why?

- You're not asking for funding or pitching investors.
- You're not running a big team — it's just you (or maybe you and a friend).
- You're testing and learning as you go — flexibility beats formality.

Most beginners waste time "planning to plan" instead of *starting small and adjusting fast.*

A simple one-pager will help you:

- Stay focused
- Make better decisions
- Explain your business clearly (to others *and* yourself)

Simple Structure: Problem → Solution → Offer → Audience → Marketing → Revenue

This format is all you need to begin. Let's break it down:

1. Problem

What problem are you solving?

Example: "Busy parents are overwhelmed by dinner planning and grocery shopping."

2. Solution

What's your solution to that problem?

"I offer easy, AI-powered weekly meal plans with a grocery list."

3. Offer

What exactly do you sell or provide? (Product, service, or content.)

"A $15/month subscription to receive new plans each Sunday."

4. Audience

Who are you helping? Be specific.

"Parents aged 30–45, working full-time, with 2+ kids at home."

5. Marketing

How will they find out about you?

"Instagram tips, email newsletter, local parenting groups."

6. Revenue

How will you make money? What's your pricing?

"$15/month per subscriber. Goal: 100 customers = $1,500/month."

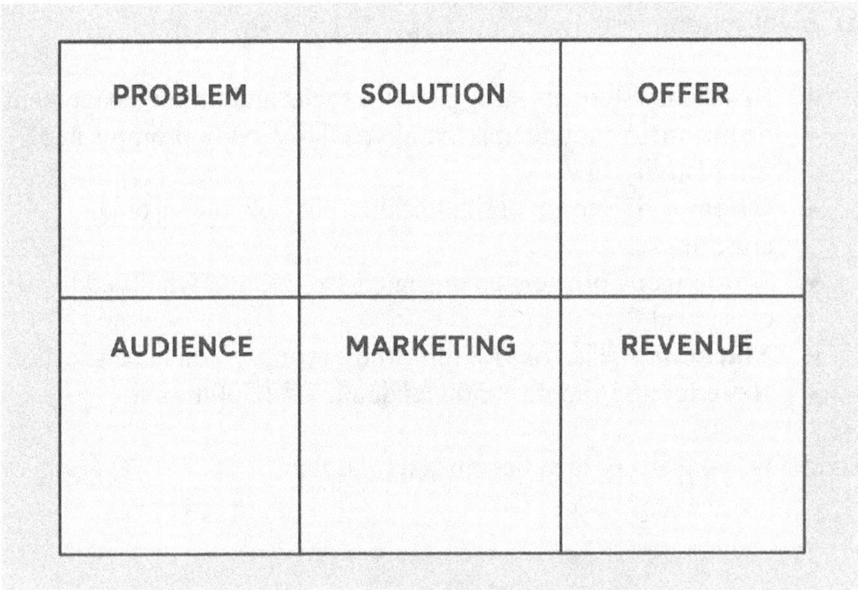

AI Prompt: "Help Me Create a Simple Business Plan for My [Type] Business"

Open ChatGPT and try this exact prompt:

“Help me create a simple business plan for a one-person business that [what your business does]. Keep it to 1 page and use this structure: Problem, Solution, Offer, Audience, Marketing, Revenue.”

You can also add:

“Give me 3 tagline ideas and a short mission statement.”

Example:

“Help me create a business plan for a digital product that helps college students stay focused using AI-guided study tools.”

AI might return:

- **Problem:** Students struggle with focus and time management
- **Solution:** A mobile app that gives daily study prompts and productivity tips
- **Offer:** A $5/month digital productivity planner + email coaching
- **Audience:** College students aged 18–24, overwhelmed by class load
- **Marketing:** TikTok, Reddit Study groups, YouTube shorts
- **Revenue:** $5/month × 500 students = $2,500/month

Suddenly, your fuzzy idea becomes a real plan.

Template Included: Fill-in-the-Blank Plan

Here's your fill-in-the-blank version to copy or print:

One-Page Business Plan Template

- **Problem:**
  The people I want to help struggle with...
- **Solution:**
  My business solves this by...
- **Offer:**
  I will sell or provide... (product, service, content)
- **Audience:**
  My ideal customer is... (age, type, lifestyle)
- **Marketing:**
  I'll reach them through...
- **Revenue:**
  I'll charge... and my first goal is to earn...

Fill this out with real words. Doesn't have to be perfect — just *real*.

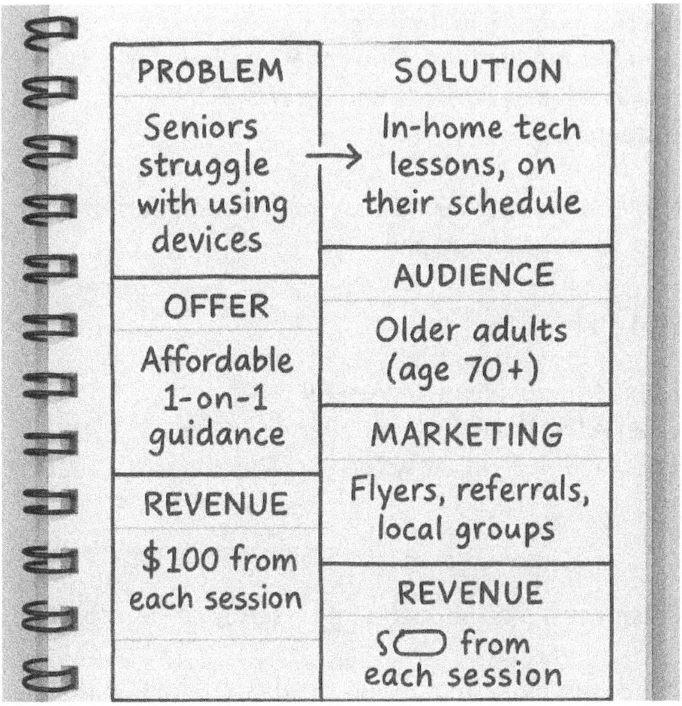

Real-World Example: Ravi's One-Page Freelance Plan

What happened:
Ravi wanted to offer freelance video editing, but had no idea how to plan it out. He was overwhelmed by all the "business advice" online.

He opened ChatGPT and used this exact prompt:

"Help me write a one-page business plan for a freelance video editing service that helps YouTubers."

Within minutes, he had:

- A clear offer: monthly video packages
- A price point: $300/month
- A target market: new YouTubers with under 10k followers
- A way to market: DMs and before/after samples on Instagram

He printed the plan and taped it next to his computer. It reminded him of who he was helping and *why*.

What went right:

- Kept it small, clear, and useful
- Used AI to break through overwhelm
- Took action right away (he got 2 clients in his first month)

This plan isn't just a document — it's your map.

It doesn't need to be perfect. It just needs to point in a direction that feels real and possible. You'll adjust as you learn.

In the next chapter, we'll help you *set up* your business — email, phone, website, and more — without drowning in tech stress.

Let's bring your plan to life.

NEXT STEPS

- Use the 6-part plan structure to clarify your idea
- Ask AI to write a draft plan (then tweak it!)
- Fill in your own version using the printable template
- Don't overthink — done is better than perfect
- Keep it visible — this is your guide

Next up: Chapter 7 — Setting Up Your Business (Without Tech Stress)
From legal basics to setting up your email and website, we'll make the setup process super doable — even if tech isn't your thing.

Chapter 7: Setting Up Your Business (Without Tech Stress)

Introduction

You've got a clear idea. A name you like. A one-page plan that makes sense. Now it's time to *actually set up your business.*

This is the part that usually makes people freeze. "Wait — do I need a license?" "How do I get a business email?" "What about a website?!"

Breathe. You don't need to know everything right away. This chapter will walk you through the *minimum setup* to get legally ready, look professional, and start getting customers — without tech overwhelm.

Let's make your business *real* (but still simple).

Basic Steps to Get Your Business Legally Ready (Local Tips, Registration)

Every country, state, and city has its own rules, so check your local guidelines — but here are the most common steps:

Step 1: Choose Your Business Structure

For most beginners, this is usually:

- **Sole Proprietorship** (default, easiest to start)
- **LLC (Limited Liability Company)** — adds protection but may have fees

TIP: You can always start as a sole proprietor and switch later.

Step 2: Register Your Business Name

You may need to file a *DBA* (Doing Business As) if your brand name is different from your personal name.

Step 3: Check for Permits (if needed)

Most online businesses don't need special permits. But if you're selling food, offering physical services, or working locally — check with your city or state.

Step 4: Get an EIN (for U.S.) or Tax ID (elsewhere)

This is like a business version of a social security number — helpful for taxes and opening a business bank account. It's *free* to get through official government sites.

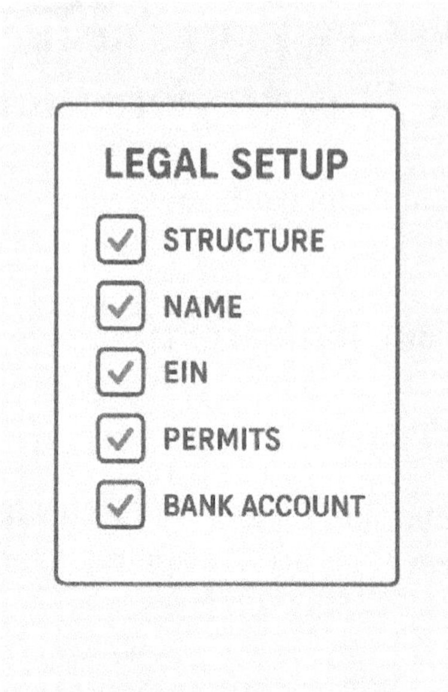

Easy Tools to Set Up Your Business Email, Phone Number, and Invoicing

You don't need a big tech setup — just a few tools to look legit and stay organized.

📧 Business Email

- **Option 1:** Use Gmail with your name (e.g. yournamebiz@gmail.com) to start
- **Option 2:** Use Google Workspace to get a branded email (e.g. hello@yourbiz.com)

📞 Business Phone Number

- Try **Google Voice** (free in the U.S.)
- Or use **OpenPhone** or **Grasshopper** to get a dedicated business line

📄 Invoicing + Payments

- **PayPal Business** or **Stripe** are great to send professional invoices
- Use **Wave**, **FreshBooks**, or **HoneyBook** to track payments

These tools help you stay separate from your personal life — and they make you look way more trustworthy to clients.

AI Assistance: Use ChatGPT to Help You Write Your Business Intro and Service List

Let's face it — writing about yourself and your business is tough. But AI makes it *way* easier.

Prompt for a Business Intro (Website or Social Bio)

"Can you write a short, friendly business intro for a solo business that helps [audience] with [problem]? Make it sound confident and helpful."

Example Output:

"I help busy parents stay organized and stress-free with weekly digital planners designed just for family life."

Prompt for a Service or Product List

"Here are the services I want to offer: [list]. Can you write a short, clear description for each one that sounds beginner-friendly?"

Pro Tip: Ask for:

- Bullet points
- A version for your homepage
- A shorter version for your Instagram bio

No-Code Website Tools to Use (Carrd, Notion, Squarespace Basics)

You do *not* need to hire a web developer or spend $5,000 on a fancy website. You just need a page that tells people:

- Who you are
- What you offer
- How to contact or buy from you

3 Beginner-Friendly, No-Code Website Tools

1. Carrd

- Super simple, one-page websites
- Free to start
- Great for link-in-bio or service-based businesses

2. Notion (with Super or Potion)

- Looks like a digital dashboard
- Great for creators, course makers, or newsletter-style setups

3. Squarespace

- Clean, easy templates
- Includes hosting + domain options
- Ideal if you want more design flexibility

Use AI to write your homepage content, then paste it in and go live — even in one afternoon.

Bonus Prompt:

"Can you write a one-page homepage for a business that offers [your product/service] to [your audience]?"

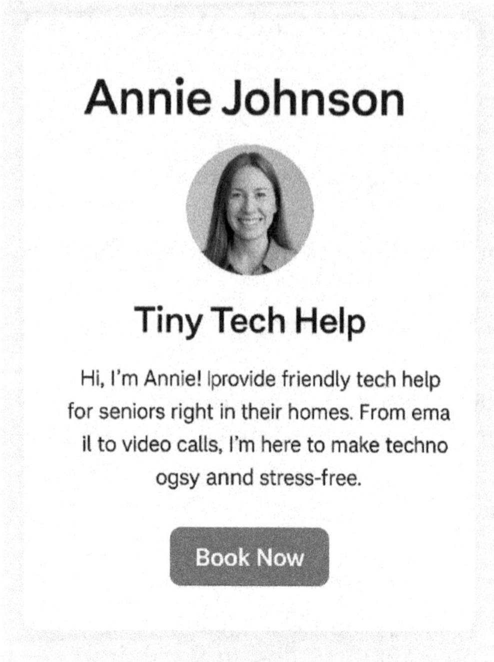

A one-page wesebrata
for Carrd

Real-World Example: Maya's Declutter Coaching Website

What happened:
Maya offered 1-on-1 virtual sessions to help people declutter their homes. She wanted a simple online presence but felt totally lost.

She used:

- **ChatGPT** to write her homepage
- **Carrd** to build a one-page site with her photo, services, and a "Book Now" button
- **Google Voice** for her business phone number
- **Stripe** to collect payments

Her website was live in *one day* — and she got her first booking by the end of the week.

What went right:

- She didn't overcomplicate
- She used the tools available
- She let AI take care of the tech-y stuff

Starting your business doesn't mean becoming a tech wizard. It just means putting a few small systems in place — so you can start *serving people, making money,* and building momentum.

In the next chapter, you'll actually *create your first offer or product* — and test it the smart way (no need to build everything upfront).

NEXT STEPS

- Handle your basic legal setup (structure, name, tax ID)
- Use simple tools for your email, phone, and payments
- Let AI write your intro, service list, or homepage copy
- Publish a one-page site using Carrd, Notion, or Squarespace
- Remember: done is better than perfect — launch fast, fix later

Next up: Chapter 8 — Create Your First Offer, Product, or Service
You'll learn how to go from idea to income with a test-first approach — and how to use AI to write your product descriptions and pricing copy.

Chapter 8: Create Your First Offer, Product, or Service

Introduction

This is where your idea becomes real — and *starts making money.* But not by building a giant product or spending months creating something. That's where most people get stuck.

We're not here to build. We're here to *test.*

Your goal in this chapter is to create a **starter offer** — something small, clear, and useful that lets people say "yes" (or "not yet") so you can learn fast, improve quickly, and grow with confidence.

Let's get something out into the world that people can see, buy, or try.

Start Simple: Don't Build — Test

You might be tempted to build a full website, write an entire course, or launch a digital store with 20 products. **Don't.**

Instead, ask:

- "What's the smallest version of this that I could offer right now?"
- "Can I *talk* about it before I build it?"
- "Can I create a *preview* version before going all in?"

Your first offer is just a way to:

- Get feedback
- Learn what people want
- See who's interested

Think of it like a pop-up stand — not a brick-and-mortar store.

Test-first mindset:

- *Idea → Offer → Feedback → Improve → Build more*

That's how you avoid wasting time on things no one buys — and start building something people actually want.

Full Product	First Offer
Full course	1:1 call
Full ebook	Starter checklist
Full service	One-time session

Examples: Coaching, Ebook, Digital Product, Template, Consultation, Newsletter

Not sure what to offer? Here are beginner-friendly formats you can create with **zero tech skills**:

1. Mini Coaching or Consulting

Offer a 30-minute call where you help solve a specific problem.

Example: "Need help organizing your home office? Let's fix it together in 30 minutes."

2. Downloadable Template or Tool

Use Google Docs, Canva, or Notion to make a checklist, script, or planner.

Example: "My 3-day budget reset guide — free with email signup."

3. Micro Ebook or Guide

Write 3–5 pages with ChatGPT's help and save as a PDF.

Example: "How I Got 3 Freelance Clients in 7 Days — My Real Process."

4. Email Newsletter or Tips Series

Start a free or paid newsletter and share advice regularly.

Example: "Weekly calm for overwhelmed moms — 5-minute reads to reset your week."

5. Simple Subscription

Offer something recurring: new recipes, stock photos, social post templates, etc.

Example: "3 AI-written Instagram captions delivered every week — $9/month."

The key is to **keep it useful, focused, and easy to explain**.

AI Prompt Ideas: "What Could I Offer as a Beginner in [Industry]?"

If you're stuck thinking, "But what can *I* offer?", let AI help you figure it out.

Here are some prompts you can use in ChatGPT:

General:

"I'm just starting out in [industry or niche]. What kind of small, beginner-friendly product or service could I offer to test demand?"

With context:

"I love organizing, and I've helped friends clean up their home offices. Can you give me 5 simple service ideas I could offer online?"

If you want digital products:

"What kind of digital download or low-cost offer could I create for people who want help with [problem]?"

AI may suggest:

- A 1-page PDF checklist
- A "mini audit" or review via email
- A short ebook or starter toolkit
- A consultation call
- A pre-written template bundle

Pick *one*, try it, and adjust from there.

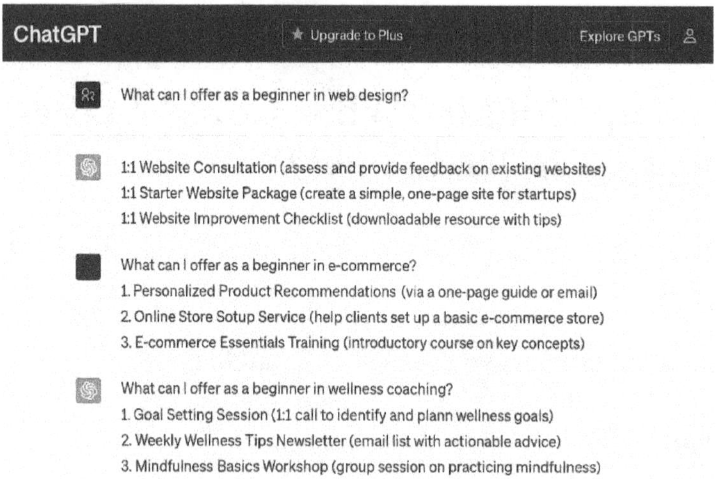

Use ChatGPT to Write Your Product Description, Benefits, and Pricing Test Copy

Once you have an offer idea, you'll need a short description that tells people what it is, why it matters, and what they'll get.

Here's how to get AI to write it for you.

Prompt:

"Can you write a friendly product description for [describe your offer], including who it helps, how it works, and 3 benefits?"

Example Output:

"Struggle to stay focused when working from home? My 30-minute Focus Reset Call helps you declutter your day, block distractions, and build a mini routine that sticks. Perfect for freelancers, creatives, and remote workers who want more peace and productivity."

Now ask:

"Can you write a short version for a website or social media post?"
"Can you give me 3 headline ideas and a call-to-action?"

Use this content in your:

- Website
- Instagram bio
- First offer email
- DM messages
- Test landing page

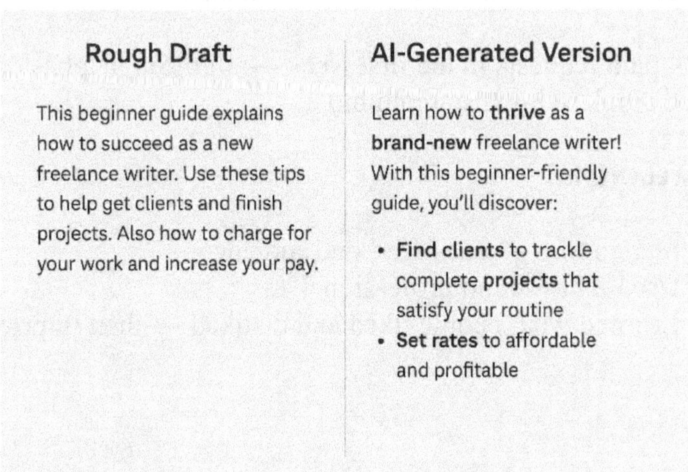

Real-World Example: Omar's "Fix My Resume" Offer

What happened:
Omar wanted to help people land better jobs but didn't know where to start. He used ChatGPT to brainstorm beginner offers.

AI suggested:

- Resume reviews
- LinkedIn profile audits
- 15-minute Q&A calls for job seekers

Omar picked one:

"Fix My Resume — One-Time Tune-Up for $35"

He used AI to write:

- A short offer description
- 3 benefit points
- An FAQ section
- A call-to-action: "Send me your resume and I'll send back personalized improvements in 48 hours."

He got 4 paid requests in the first week — all through a basic Notion page and a link in his Instagram bio.

What went right:

- Started *tiny* — one offer, one audience
- Used AI to sound professional
- Learned what people liked and disliked — then improved

You don't need to wait until everything's perfect. Just create something small, helpful, and honest — and see what happens.

In the next chapter, we'll help you actually launch it. Calmly. Softly. Smartly. Because launching isn't about going big — it's about *beginning.*

NEXT STEPS

- Pick a small offer: one idea, one format, one audience
- Use AI to explore and shape your offer description
- Keep it simple, useful, and easy to say yes to
- Don't build a big product — *test* a little version
- Share it with 3 people and ask for honest feedback

Next up: Chapter 9 — Launch Your Business (Soft, Calm, and Smart)
We'll walk through your first soft launch — how to reach out, what to say, and how AI can help you write your first email or social post.

Chapter 9: Launch Your Business (Soft, Calm, and Smart)

Introduction

The word *"launch"* can feel intimidating. Like you're supposed to plan a huge event, make everything perfect, and tell the world all at once.

Let's take the pressure off.

A launch isn't a big moment. It's just your first *invitation.*

It can be a quiet post, a friendly message, or a soft email to people who already know you. In this chapter, you'll learn how to **launch simply, calmly, and smartly** — without needing a giant audience or perfect setup.

We'll also show you how to use AI to write your launch content, reach out with confidence, and attract your first real customer or follower.

What Launching *Really* Means (Not Perfection, Just Start)

You don’t need:

- A big following
- A polished website
- A perfect product

You *do* need:

- A real offer
- A few people to share it with
- A way for them to say yes

That’s it.

Launching is simply the moment you say:

“Hey — I’ve got something that might help. Want to check it out?”

It’s the point where your idea leaves your head and enters someone else’s world.

Soft launch > Silent launch > No launch.

How to Get Your First Customer or Follower

Forget ads, funnels, or paid promotions. Focus on people who already know, like, or trust you.

Here's your starting point:

- Friends and family
- Former coworkers or classmates
- People in a relevant community (Facebook group, forum, local group)
- Your small social media following

Ask yourself:

- Who has this problem?
- Who do I already know that fits my ideal customer profile?
- Who might know *someone else* who needs this?

You don't have to "sell" — you're inviting, sharing, and offering to help.

Example intro message:

"Hey! I just started offering a [service/product] that helps [audience] with [problem]. Would love to hear what you think or if you know anyone who might be into it!"

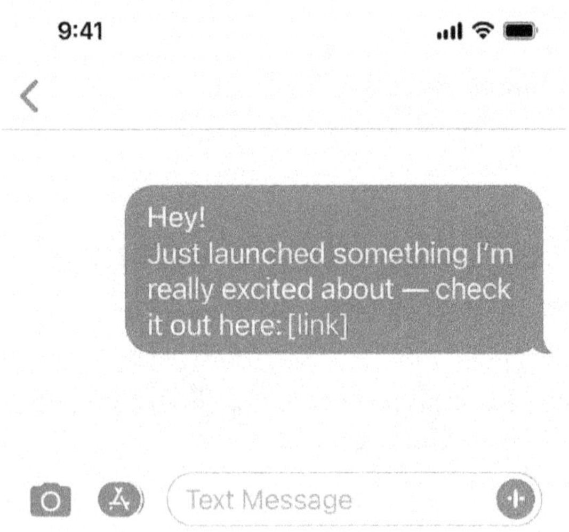

Simple Ways to Launch: Email, Social, One-on-One Message

You don't need a full campaign. Try one of these soft-start methods:

1. Direct Message (DM) or Text

- Personal, private, easy
- Great for friends, former coworkers, or warm leads

2. Email

- Short and friendly
- Even 5–10 people is a great start
- Subject line idea: *"Quick question — would this be helpful to you?"*

3. Instagram / Facebook / LinkedIn Post

- Use a photo of you, your work, or your screen
- Share your *why* and how you help
- Include a soft call-to-action: *"DM me if you want to try it out!"*

TIP: Start with the place where you feel most comfortable.

AI Tools: Write Your Launch Post, First Promo Email, and CTA with ChatGPT

Use ChatGPT to help you *say the right thing* — even if writing isn't your thing.

Here are some starter prompts:

🎯 Launch Email

"Can you write a friendly launch email announcing my new [product/service] for [audience], including what it is, how it helps, and a clear CTA?"

Example Output:

"Exciting news! I just created something to help busy freelancers stay focused and organized — my new Productivity Reset Kit. If you're feeling scattered, this might be just what you need."

🗣 Social Post

"Write a short and casual launch announcement for Instagram, including a photo caption and a CTA."

AI might suggest:

"I've been working on this quietly… and it's finally here! 💡 A little tool to help creatives stay on track and avoid burnout. Want to try it? DM me 'reset' and I'll send you the link."

📱 Call-to-Action (CTA)

"Write 3 versions of a soft CTA to include at the end of a post or email."

Examples:

- "Curious? DM me to check it out."
- "Want early access? Just reply 'YES.'"
- "First 5 people get it free — hit reply if you're in."

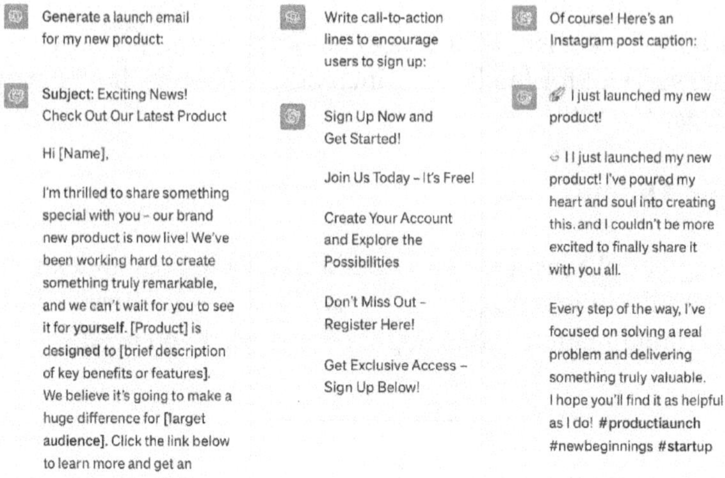

Real-World Example: Dani's Soft Launch Success

What happened:
Dani created a Notion-based budget tracker for students. Instead of trying to launch with ads or a fancy website, she:

- Sent a text to 5 friends
- Posted on her IG stories: *"Built this tool I wish I had in college — want to try it?"*
- Asked ChatGPT to help write a short offer description

Within 3 days:

- 9 people had signed up
- 2 gave her feedback
- 1 offered to *pay* for a premium version

What went right:

- She kept it personal
- Focused on her audience's problem
- Let AI take care of the writing

She didn't "go viral." She went *real.* And that's what works when you're just starting.

A launch doesn't have to be loud — just *real*. Focus on people, not perfection. Use tools that reduce stress. And remember, your very first sale or follower is the *hardest* — and also the most exciting.

Let's make it happen.

NEXT STEPS

- Choose your calmest, clearest way to launch
- Write a message, post, or email using AI
- Share it with a few people who already trust you
- Don't chase scale — chase connection
- Celebrate your first "yes," no matter how small

Next up: Chapter 10 — Marketing Without Overwhelm
You'll learn how to start marketing in just 15 minutes a day — without burnout — and how AI can help create and batch your content.

Chapter 10: Marketing Without Overwhelm

Introduction

Marketing is one of the most misunderstood — and most feared — parts of starting a business.

Many people think marketing means:

- Constantly being on social media
- Sounding fake or salesy
- Spending hours you don't have creating content

But here's the truth:

Marketing is simply helping the right people find you — in a way that feels good to *you*.

This chapter will teach you how to:

- Understand what marketing *really* is (in plain language)
- Start marketing in just 15 minutes a day
- Use AI to help generate content ideas, write faster, and batch with ease
- Use tools like ChatGPT, Canva, and Repurpose.io (without needing to be a "creator")

You don't have to become an influencer. You just need to show up — clearly, calmly, and consistently.

What Is Marketing, Really? A Slow Learner's Approach

Let's break it down:

Marketing = Visibility + Value + Invitation

You don't have to impress people. You just have to:

- Let them know you exist
- Show them how you can help
- Invite them to take the next step

If you've helped someone, shared a tip, or explained your offer clearly — you've already started marketing.

Think of it like this:

- If launching is "opening your door,"
- Marketing is "hanging up a friendly sign and waving at people passing by."

Marketing is not hype. It's **helpful communication**.

How to Start Marketing in Just 15 Minutes/Day

Marketing doesn't need to eat your schedule. In fact, many beginner-friendly businesses grow by doing **one tiny action per day.**

Here's a realistic starter plan:

🕒 15-Minute Daily Marketing Practice

Day 1: Share something useful
→ A tip, tool, or lesson related to your offer

Day 2: Tell a story
→ Why you started your business or a challenge you've faced

Day 3: Show your offer
→ Post or email explaining what you do and how to try it

Day 4: Answer a question
→ Pick something a customer might ask and respond with value

Day 5: Invite action
→ CTA: "Want this? DM me," "Sign up here," or "Book a spot"

Repeat. Adapt. And breathe.

Even 2–3 posts, messages, or emails per week can build momentum fast.

Content Ideas + Batching With AI Help (Emails, Posts, Blog, Scripts)

Don't try to create new content every day. Instead, **batch** a week's worth in one sitting — then schedule or drip it out.

AI can help you:

- Brainstorm post ideas
- Write drafts
- Turn one idea into multiple formats (a post, an email, a story, etc.)

Use This Prompt to Plan 1 Week of Content:

"Create 5 beginner-friendly content ideas for a solo business that helps [audience] with [problem]. Include ideas for social posts, short emails, and tips."

AI Might Return:

1. "5 Quick Fixes for [Problem]" (Instagram carousel)
2. "Why I Started This Business" (Email)
3. "What My First Client Taught Me" (LinkedIn post)
4. "Common Mistakes People Make With [Topic]" (IG reel)
5. "Want to Try It?" (Soft CTA with offer details)

You can then say:

"Turn idea #1 into a short caption and an email draft."

ChatGPT

A Content Idea Expanded into Three Formats

Content Idea: I tried something new and saw an exciting result

Social Caption: I tried something new... and guess what? It paid off! Excited to share this journey and the impact it's had. Stay tuned for more! #Innovation #Growth

Email Draft: Subject: I Tried Something New and It Paid Off!
Hi everyone,
I'm excited to let you in on a little experiment I recently conducted. I stepped out of my comfort zone to try something new, and the results were better than I could have hoped. In this email, I'll walk you through what I did and how it led to an amazing outcome.

Blog Intro: I'm a firm believer that stepping outside your comfort zone can lead to incredible growth. Recently, I put this belief to the test by trying

---

AI Tools: ChatGPT, Canva, Repurpose.io for Beginners

Here are 3 tools that make content creation feel *lightweight*:

1. ChatGPT

- Plan your content calendar
- Draft captions, headlines, and CTAs
- Edit posts to sound more natural or professional

2. Canva

- Create clean, branded visuals for your posts, flyers, and PDFs
- Use templates so you don't start from scratch
- Add your logo, colors, and photo — done in minutes

3. Repurpose.io

- Take one video (like a Reel or TikTok) and convert it into 10 formats
- Saves time by auto-resharing your content across platforms
- Ideal if you create *any* short video or audio content

You don't have to use all 3 — just pick the one that matches your style. Writing? Use ChatGPT. Visual? Use Canva. Talking? Try Repurpose.

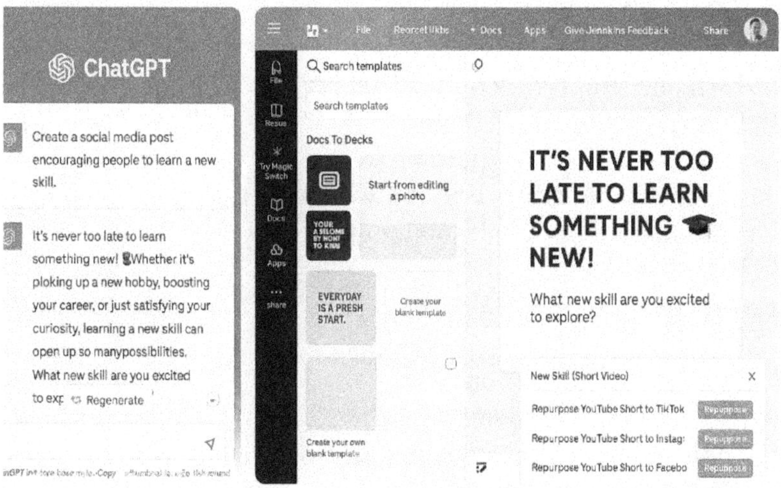

Real-World Example: Jenna's 15-Minute Marketing Habit

What happened:
Jenna ran a side hustle selling Canva templates. But she hated social media and froze every time she tried to "market."

She used ChatGPT to:

- Plan 5 weekly content ideas
- Write captions that felt human
- Script a short story post about why she started

She used Canva to:

- Batch 3 weeks of social posts in one sitting
- Create a "launch announcement" template to reuse
- Make a lead magnet for her email list

She used Repurpose.io to:

- Turn one simple video into 3 IG reels, a YouTube short, and a Pinterest pin

Now Jenna spends less than 1 hour a week on marketing — and makes consistent monthly sales without stress.

What worked:

- Tiny, repeatable actions
- AI for writing support
- Tools that simplified design and repurposing

You don't need to become a marketing expert. You just need a few tools, a simple routine, and a message that makes someone say, "That's for me."

Your job isn't to be everywhere. It's to show up *where it matters most* — consistently and kindly.

NEXT STEPS

- Redefine marketing as helpful visibility
- Pick 1–2 tools to support your style (writing, visuals, or voice)
- Use AI to plan and draft a week of content in 15–30 minutes
- Share something this week — even one post or email
- Build momentum gently, without pressure

Next up: Chapter 11 — Automate What You Hate (No Code Required)
We'll show you how to take the tasks you repeat (like emails, confirmations, or reminders) and set them to run on autopilot — with easy tools and no tech headaches.

Chapter 11: Automate What You Hate (No Code Required)

Introduction

Let's face it — running a business means doing a *lot* of repetitive stuff. Scheduling calls. Sending confirmations. Following up with clients. Answering the same questions again and again.

Sound familiar?

The good news is:

You can automate most of those tasks — even if you're not "techy" — and it won't cost you much time or money.

This chapter is about **working smarter, not harder**. You'll learn:

- What kinds of tasks you can automate
- Which beginner-safe tools to use (no coding required)
- How AI can help you write, tag, and trigger messages
- And how to set it all up in a step-by-step flow

Ready to save time and energy? Let's go.

What Tasks You Can Automate (Scheduling, Follow-Ups, Confirmations)

Start by asking:
What do I keep doing over and over?

If you've done it more than 3 times, chances are — you can automate it.

Common beginner-friendly automations:

- **Client scheduling:** Set your availability and let people book themselves
- **Payment + confirmation:** Send auto-confirmation after a purchase
- **Email follow-ups:** Remind someone they left their cart or didn't finish signing up
- **Onboarding:** Automatically send your welcome email or guide after someone joins
- **Contact form → Email sequence:** When someone fills out your form, they get an instant reply and added to your email list

Zapier, Tally, and Other Beginner-Safe Tools

You don't need to code. These tools are drag-and-drop simple — made for beginners who just want to *get things done.*

☑ Tools We Recommend:

Zapier

- Connects 2+ apps (e.g. form → Google Sheet, or Gmail → Notion)
- Use pre-built "Zaps" like:
  - "New form → send thank you email"
  - "Stripe payment → add client to CRM"

Tally Forms

- Free, no-code form builder (like Google Forms, but prettier)
- Great for intake forms, lead captures, and onboarding
- Connects with Zapier to trigger automations

Calendly or SavvyCal

- Set your availability and let people book time without email back-and-forth
- Auto-sends confirmations and reminders

MailerLite / ConvertKit

- Beginner-friendly email marketing
- Automate welcome emails, sequences, and lead magnets

You don't need to set up everything at once. Just start with *one* task you do every week — and automate it away.

AI Helps With Writing Emails, Tagging Leads, Sending Messages

AI isn't just for writing blog posts — it's also perfect for helping you create automation content.

Prompt ideas to write automation emails:

1. Welcome Email After Sign-Up

"Write a friendly welcome email for someone who just signed up for my free [guide/workshop/offer]. Make it warm and personal."

2. Follow-Up Reminder Email

"Write a short follow-up for someone who filled out my form but hasn't booked yet. Keep it kind and helpful."

3. Post-Purchase Confirmation

"Write an email that thanks a new customer for purchasing [product] and tells them what happens next."

Bonus Prompt:

"Create 3 email templates for onboarding new clients in my [type of business]. Keep them short, clear, and friendly."

You can also ask:

- "How should I tag leads based on what form they filled out?"
- "How can I personalize emails using fields like name or service?"

AI + automation = clarity + consistency — even while you sleep.

Automation Setup Flow: Step-by-Step With Screenshots

Let's walk through a sample automation flow. This one uses **Tally + Zapier + Gmail** to send a welcome email when someone fills out your contact form.

🛠 Step-by-Step:

1. **Create a Tally form**
   → Ask for name, email, and what they're interested in
2. **Connect Tally to Zapier**
   → Use the "New submission" trigger
3. **Add an action: Send email via Gmail**
   → Paste in your AI-written welcome message
4. **(Optional) Add a second action: Add contact to MailerLite list**
   → Begin a drip campaign or tag for follow-up

That's it. One form → personalized welcome → email list → done.

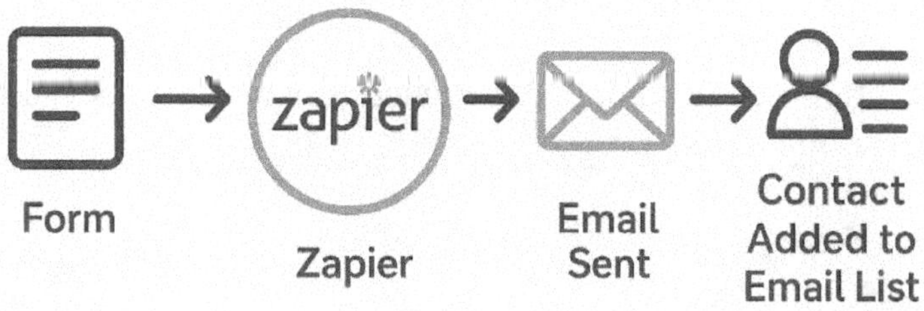

You can repeat this flow for:

- Appointment reminders
- Payment confirmations
- Lead magnet delivery
- "Nudge" emails for people who didn't complete something

Real-World Example: Andre's Client Booking Automation

What happened:
Andre offered coaching calls — but hated manually booking appointments, sending reminders, and writing follow-up emails.

Here's what he automated:

- **Calendly**: Set availability + booking link
- **Zapier**: When someone books, add them to Notion client tracker
- **ChatGPT**: Wrote:
  - Confirmation email
  - Reminder email
  - Post-call feedback request

Now his clients get a smooth experience — and Andre doesn't spend hours on admin work.

What worked:

- One simple workflow at a time
- AI for all the writing
- Clear setup, tested once — now runs on autopilot

Automation isn't about building a robot business. It's about freeing you from the stuff you *don't* want to do — so you can spend more time on what you love.

Even just automating **one task this week** can change the way your business feels.

NEXT STEPS

- Pick one task you repeat every week (like booking, follow-ups, or emails)
- Use Tally or Calendly to collect info
- Use Zapier to trigger the next step
- Let AI write your email or message content
- Test the flow once — then enjoy the time you just saved

Next up: Chapter 12 — Grow at Your Own Pace (And Don't Burn Out)
You'll learn how to set real goals, track your progress, and grow your business without losing your mind — all with a little AI support.

Chapter 12: Grow at Your Own Pace (And Don't Burn Out)

Introduction

You've come so far — and we mean that. Whether you've launched, tested your first offer, or are just beginning to see yourself as a real business owner… we're proud of you.

But now comes the part no one talks about enough:

How do you grow your business without growing your stress?

Too many brilliant beginners burn out trying to "scale" too fast, compare themselves to others, or chase goals that don't actually fit their life.

This final chapter is about **sustainable, soul-friendly growth** — the kind that works for *you*, on your terms. We'll help you:

- Set simple, achievable goals
- Check your progress without judgment
- Navigate fear, doubt, or burnout
- And build a gentle 3-month growth roadmap, supported by AI

Let's grow — not with pressure, but with purpose.

Setting Goals You Can Actually Achieve

The best goals aren't big — they're *real.*

They match your energy, your schedule, your lifestyle, and your current season of life. Growth should stretch you, not strangle you.

The 3-Part Goal Check:

Before setting any goal, ask:

1. **Is this goal specific and simple?**
   → Not "grow on Instagram," but "post 2 helpful tips per week."
2. **Does this goal fit into my week — without stealing joy?**
   → Not "write a course in 2 weeks," but "outline 3 lesson ideas this month."
3. **Will this goal move me closer to helping more people?**
   → Focus on *service*, not just stats.

Prompt for AI Goal Support:

"Help me set 3 realistic business goals for the next 30 days. I'm currently offering [product/service] and have [X] hours/week to work on it."

You can also ask:

- "Help me choose between two priorities."
- "Break this big goal into weekly steps I can actually follow."

Hello! To set realistic, heart-centered goals for your business, let's identify what's achievable and meaningful for you.

- Generate $2,000 in monthly revenue
- Help 5 new clients
- Launch a website
- Post on social media regularly

Does this look good to you?

Yes, this looks great!

CF

Great! Let's break your goals into weekly milestones:

1. Reach out to 5 prospects
2. Onboard your first client
3. Finish your homepage
4. Schedule 3 posts for the week

How to Review Progress and Improve — With AI Support

Reflection helps you grow smarter — not harder. But many entrepreneurs never stop to review what's working.

Take 15 minutes each week to ask:

- What felt good this week?
- What did I learn from what didn't work?
- What one thing would I improve or try differently?

AI can help here too.

Prompt:

"Help me reflect on my business this week. I launched [X], tried [Y], and felt [Z]. What should I focus on next week?"

ChatGPT can help you:

- Spot patterns
- Pull out wins you forgot to celebrate
- Suggest micro-adjustments that save time and energy

And don't just track sales — track **energy**, **confidence**, and **connection.** Those matter just as much.

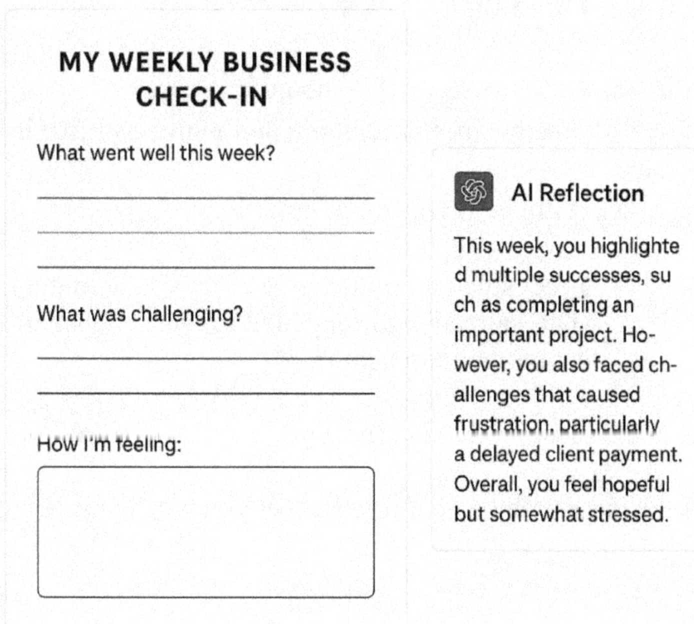

What to Do If You're Stuck, Scared, or Burned Out

This part's real — and important.

At some point, you'll hit a wall. You'll feel tired, doubtful, or like everyone else has it figured out but you.

Here's what we want you to remember:

You're not behind. You're not broken. You're building.

And sometimes building includes rest, reflection, or reevaluating.

Gentle Reset Checklist:

- ☑ Take one full day off — no guilt
- ☑ Talk to a business friend or community (not just in your head)
- ☑ Ask AI to help you zoom out:

> "I feel stuck in my business. Can you help me list what's already working, and suggest one small step to feel momentum again?"

Sometimes the most productive thing you can do is pause.

Let your business breathe, and it will meet you when you're ready.

The 3-Month Growth Roadmap: What to Add Next, and When

You don't need a 5-year plan. You need a 3-month map that aligns with your pace and values.

Here's a sample roadmap to build on what you've done:

Month 1 – Stabilize
Goal: Keep things light, steady, and consistent

- Refine your first offer
- Post or email once a week
- Automate 1 new task
- Rest more than you think you need

Month 2 – Grow Gently
Goal: Add a second way to deliver value

- Create a lead magnet or freebie
- Grow your email list by 20–50 people
- Reach out for 1 collaboration or shoutout
- Try a new content format (like video or blog)

Month 3 – Expand (if you want to)
Goal: Scale *without stress*

- Raise your prices (even by $5)
- Launch a second small offer or product
- Repurpose content into an ebook, course, or workshop
- Let AI help build a 3-month content bank

Use AI to adjust this plan:

"Here's where I am with my business: [describe briefly]. Can you help me plan the next 3 months based on my energy level and current results?"

This isn't a race. It's a rhythm.

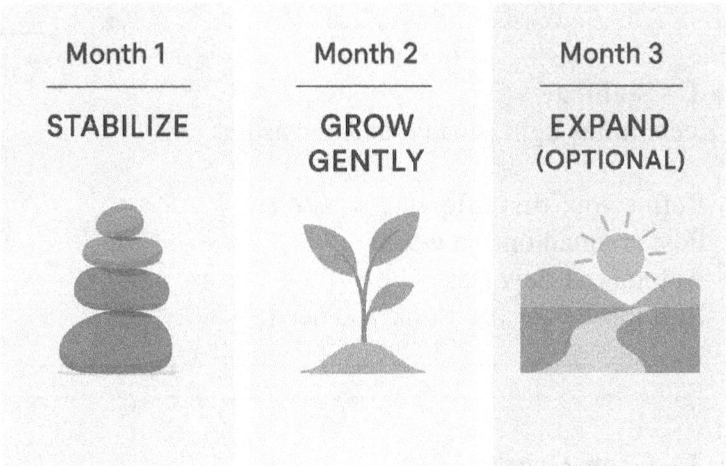

Real-World Closing: Alex's Peaceful Pivot

What happened:
Alex started offering career coaching but quickly got overwhelmed. She was trying to grow fast, build a blog, post daily, and automate everything at once.

She hit burnout — hard.

She paused. Came back slowly. Used ChatGPT to help her:

- Simplify her offer
- Set 3 goals for the next 30 days
- Reflect weekly with gentle prompts
- Automate one email sequence instead of ten

Now Alex makes $1,200/month from just 3 coaching slots a week — and takes Fridays off. Her business fits *her life*, not the other way around.

This is the end of the book — but not the end of your journey.

You started with curiosity, and now you've got a business foundation, tools, confidence, and momentum.

Whether you grow big, stay small, pivot, pause, or expand — you're a real business owner now. And you did it **your way.**

NEXT STEPS

- Set 3 small goals that match your pace and your values
- Use AI to reflect, adjust, and support your rhythm
- Don't push — build with peace
- Let rest be part of your growth strategy
- Review your 3-month roadmap — or create one from scratch

You've got this. We believe in you. And we're cheering for everything you're becoming.

CHECK YOUR BONUS AT THE END !

Glossary: Simple Definitions for First-Time Founders

AI (Artificial Intelligence)
A smart tool that helps you get things done faster — like writing, planning, designing, or organizing. Think of it as your digital helper, not a robot replacement.

Automation
Setting up systems that run by themselves (like emails or booking confirmations), so you don't have to do the same tasks over and over again.

Batching
Doing a bunch of similar tasks all at once to save time. For example, writing 3 social posts in one sitting instead of every day.

Branding
How your business looks, feels, and sounds — your name, colors, tone, and overall vibe. It helps people recognize and remember you.

Call to Action (CTA)
A sentence that tells people what to do next, like "Click here," "Book now," or "DM me for details."

Canva
A beginner-friendly design tool to create graphics, flyers, social media posts, and more — no design experience needed.

ChatGPT
An AI tool (like the one used in this book!) that can help you write emails, brainstorm ideas, plan content, and more — just by typing a question or prompt.

Confirmation Email
An automatic message someone gets after booking, purchasing, or signing up — to say "Thanks!" and tell them what's next.

Content
Any helpful or valuable information you share — like blog posts, videos, tips, newsletters, or social media posts.

ConvertKit / MailerLite
Email tools that help you grow your list, send newsletters, and automate welcome messages. Perfect for solo founders.

DM (Direct Message)
A private message sent on platforms like Instagram, Facebook, or LinkedIn. Great for connecting with people 1-on-1.

Domain
Your website address — like *yourbusinessname.com* — that people can type in to find you online.

Digital Product
A product you sell online that doesn't require shipping — like a PDF guide, ebook, template, or online course.

Drip Campaign
A series of automated emails sent over time (like a welcome series) to build connection and trust with new subscribers.

Ebook
A short digital book — usually a PDF — that you can create and sell or give away to share knowledge or tips.

Freebie (aka Lead Magnet)
A free offer (like a guide or checklist) that someone gets in exchange for their email address. Helps grow your email list.

Landing Page
A simple one-page website that shares your offer and invites people to take one action — like signing up or buying.

Lead
Someone who's interested in what you do, but hasn't bought yet. Often someone who signed up for your email list.

Newsletter
A regular email sent to your audience — filled with tips, updates, offers, or stories.

No-Code Tool
Software that helps you build things (like websites or automations) *without needing to write code*. Super beginner-friendly.

Notion
A flexible online workspace for organizing your business — can be used for checklists, dashboards, pages, or even websites.

Offer
What you sell or provide — a product, service, or experience that solves a problem or brings value.

Onboarding
The first steps a new customer takes after signing up or buying — often includes emails, instructions, or a welcome guide.

Opt-In
When someone says "yes" to getting emails from you — often by signing up for a freebie.

Repurpose.io
A tool that helps you take one piece of content (like a video) and turn it into different formats for multiple platforms.

Schedule Tool (Calendly / SavvyCal)
Apps that let people book a time with you — no back-and-forth emailing needed. Sends auto-reminders, too.

Service-Based Business
A business where you offer your time, skills, or expertise — like coaching, consulting, or freelancing.

Soft Launch
A quiet, low-pressure way to introduce your offer to a small group — before doing a full public launch.

Solo Business / One-Person Business
A business you run by yourself, often with help from tools and automation instead of employees.

Tally
A super simple online form tool to collect info from clients, leads, or customers. Looks great and works well with automation tools.

Tagline
A short sentence that sums up what your business does and who it helps. Like a mini elevator pitch.

Template
A pre-made structure you can fill in — used for documents, graphics, emails, landing pages, and more.

Test First, Build Later
The mindset of trying a small version of your idea before creating a full product — to see what people actually want.

Value
The real help, benefit, or result your business gives someone. It's why people pay you or follow you.

Visibility
Getting seen — through posts, emails, social shares, partnerships, or showing up in search results.

Zapier
A no-code tool that connects apps together to automate your workflows. (Example: "When someone fills out this form → send them an email.")

💡 **Remember:**
You don't need to know every word. Bookmark this page. Come back when a term feels fuzzy. Use what you need — skip what you don't.

Your job isn't to memorize.
Your job is to move forward — with clarity and confidence.

You've got this. 💪

www.ingramcontent.com/pod-product-compliance
Lightning Source LLC
Chambersburg PA
CBHW071353230926
51846CB00002B/535
9781997754015

Bonus – FREE eBook Version

Want the full-color PDF version of this book?
Simply email me at **ericl@acrasolution.com** with a **screenshot of your Amazon purchase and positive review**, and I'll gladly send you your personal copy.

Thank you for taking the time to read this eBook.

Your support means more than you know. **By purchasing this book, you're directly contributing to the creation of more high-quality, practical resources** for business owners, IT leaders, and everyday professionals navigating the complex world of cybersecurity. It's because of readers like you that I can continue researching, writing, and delivering tools that make a real difference.

Whether you leave a positive review, recommend this book to a colleague, or simply apply what you've learned — **you're helping grow a stronger, safer business community. And for that, I sincerely thank you.**

At **AcraSolution**, we're committed to providing both premium services and a wide range of **free, actionable tools**. Our growing library includes documentation, articles, and step-by-step guides — designed to bring you immediate value, no strings attached.

If you need additional guidance or support, don't hesitate to visit our website www.acrasolution.com or reach out directly.

Together, we can build a more secure future.

— ***Eric LeBouthillier***
Author & Cybersecurity Strategist